# DO the PUG®

## FOOD FOR THOUGHT

SCHOLASTIC INC.

ISBN 978-1-338-60111-4

10 9 8 7 6 5 4 3 2 1      20 21 22 23 24

Printed in the U.S.A. 40
First printing 2020

Illustrated by Mercedes Padró
Written by Megan Faulkner
Book design by Becky James

# MENU

Welcome, friends!

This book is dedicated to my favorite subject —FOOD.

On the menu today —a generous helping of laffs with a side order of feels and an all-you-can-eat buffet of adorable photos of moi!

Bon appétit!

**DOUG**

FOOD

# THE FOOD GROUPS
## According to DOUG

# DOUGHNUTS
## Putting the
## DOUG in
### Doughnut

IF U NEED
THESE, THEY'LL
BE IN MY
STOMACH.

13

RULE #3: SAVE THE ENVIRONMENT— SKIP THE DISHES.

WHEN SOMEONE
OPENS A BAG OF
CHIPS . . .

34

Is there anything more adorable than a pug in a **HOT DOG** costume?

A PUG IN A HOT DOG COSTUME EATING HOT DOGS?

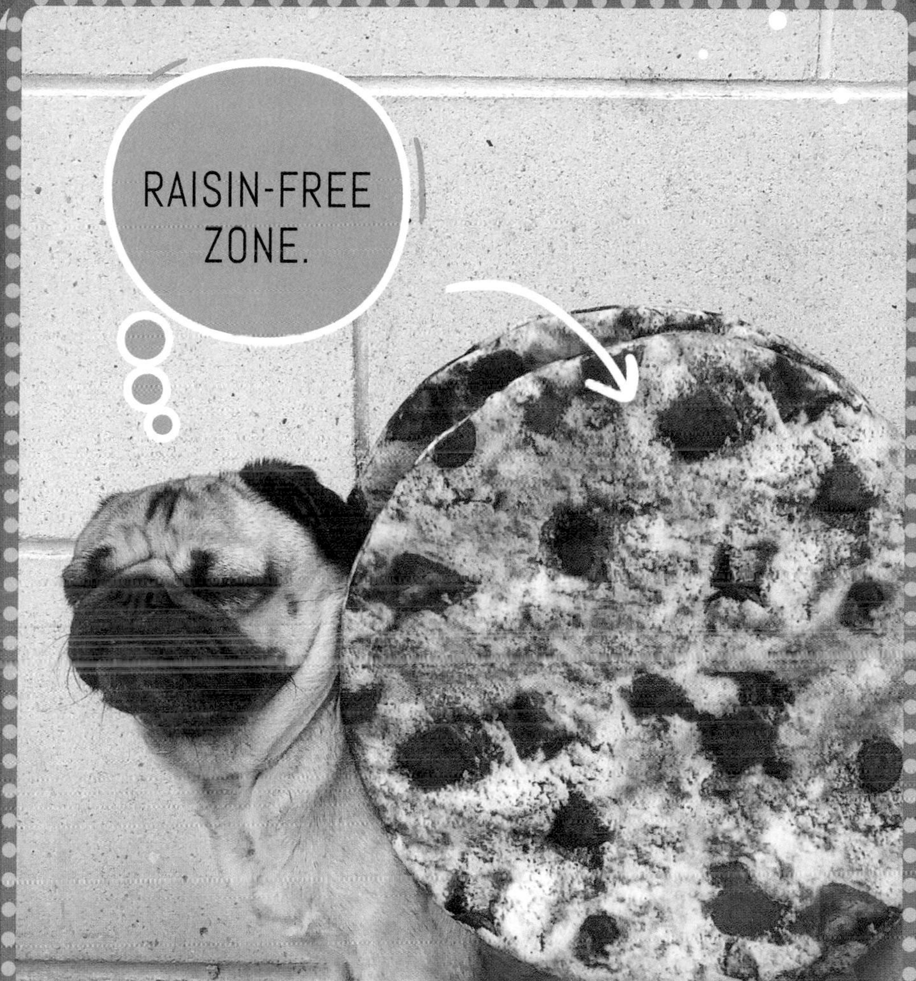
RAISIN-FREE
ZONE.

I'M MORE INTO CHUNKIES THAN SMOOTHIES.

GOOD BOYS
CLEAN UP.

HOW IT FEELS
WHEN U HAVE
LETTUCE STUCK
IN UR TEETH.

TURKEY BELONGS IN UR MOUTH, NOT ON UR HEAD.

I COULD BE SANTA.

HO HO HO

81

WELCOME TO THE NAUGHTY LIST.

THE WAY TO
MY HEART IS
THROUGH MY
STOMACH.

WHEN IN PARIS . . .

Dear Doug,

How can I make healthy food more appetizing?

— Spinachless in Spokane

Dear Spinachless,

Put it on a pizza.

Dear Doug,

I keep having nightmares. Could it be my diet?

— Sleepless in Sante Fe

Dear Sleepless,

Protect yourself from bad dreams with a sweet-treat force field.

**DOUG** ♥

P.S. Bonus! Tongue's-length proximity to midnight snacks.

Dear Doug,

Do you follow the Five-Second Rule when you drop food on the ground?

—Hungry in the Heartland

Dear Hungry,

I recommend leaving it for a good five weeks to really soak up the flavor.

DOUG

Dear Doug,

I spend too much time on the couch.
How can I be more active?

—Content on the Couch

Dear Content,

Ten reps of chip to mouth x two sets.
Refill bowl and repeat.

DOUG

P.S. If u train
hard, u can
work up to
three bowls
like me.

# TILL WE EAT AGAIN

Time for a snack break. I hope you enjoyed these slices of life! But please remember, not every animal is as full of puggitude as I am. Never feed an animal your favorite food, your least favorite food, or any human food for that matter. It may taste good, but it could make them sick! In this case, it's best to keep your food to yourself.

Till we eat again!